THE Planets
NEIGHBORS IN SPACE

An Earlybird Book
by Jeanne Bendick

Illustrated by Mike Roffe

THE MILLBROOK PRESS INC.

BROOKFIELD, CONNECTICUT

Cataloging-in-Publication Data

Bendick, Jeanne
The planets, neighbors in space.
Brookfield, CT, Millbrook Press, 1991.
32 p.; ill.: (Early Bird)
Includes index
ISBN 1-878841-51-3 pbk
1. Planets.   2. Solar system.   3. Life on other planets.

Text © 1991 Jeanne Bendick
Illustrations © 1991 Eagle Books Limited

Published by The Millbrook Press Inc, 2 Old New Milford Road, Brookfield,
Connecticut 06804, USA

Produced by Eagle Books Limited, Vigilant House, 120 Wilton Road,
London SW1V 1JZ, England

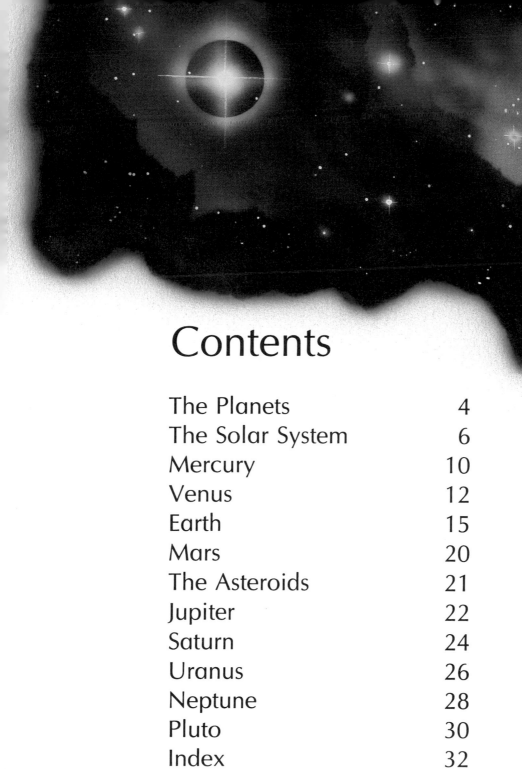

Contents

The Planets

Surely you know the numbers on your house and the name of your street.

You probably also know the name of your town or city.

Maybe you can find your country on a map.

Your house, your city, and your country are all parts of your address.

But there's even more to your address. You also live on the Planet Earth.

Planet Earth is a huge, rocky ball.

On it, there are mountains and deserts, beaches and woods. But most of the Earth is covered with water. There are oceans, lakes, rivers, and streams.

A blanket of air is wrapped around the Earth. The air around the Earth is called its **atmosphere.**

This is a picture of Planet Earth. All around the Earth is empty space. The Earth is moving through space.

4

Pluto

Mars Earth Venus

Jupiter Mercury

The Solar System

We live in a neighborhood in space that is called the **Solar System.**

Solar means "connected to the Sun."

Everything in the Solar System is connected to the Sun. It is connected by a force we cannot see. This force is called **gravity.**

The Solar System has one star. That star is the Sun. Did you know that the Sun is a star?

Stars burn. Sunlight is the light of our burning star.

The Solar System has nine planets.

They all swing around the Sun. The time it takes

The Sun

Uranus

Neptune

Saturn

for a planet to go around the Sun is its **year.** The length of each planet's year is different.

A planet's path around the Sun is called its **orbit.** Planets stay in their orbits. They are a little like trains on tracks.

While they are orbiting the Sun, planets also move in another way. They spin. Another word for spin is **rotate.** The time it takes for a planet to rotate is a **day.** The length of each planet's day is different.

When a planet rotates, part of it faces the Sun for a while. It is daytime there. It is night where the planet is turned away from the Sun.

Moons

There are many **moons** in the Solar System.
Moons are usually smaller than planets.
Moons orbit their planets the way planets orbit the Sun.
Moons also have no light of their own. Moons shine because they, too, reflect sunlight.

There are thousands of flying "rocks" in the Solar System.

These flying rocks are called **asteroids.** Asteroids are not big enough to be planets or moons. But like planets, they orbit the Sun, flying together like a flock of birds.

There are also billions of comets and meteoroids in the Solar System. **Comets** are made of ice, dust, rock, and gas. They orbit the Sun from far out in space.

Meteoroids are chunks of rock or iron. They are usually smaller than asteroids. They orbit the Sun, too.

Everything in the Solar System orbits the Sun. The Sun's gravity controls them all.

Asteroids

Mercury

Earth

Mercury

Mercury is a planet in the Solar System.

Every planet in the Solar System has its own address.

Mercury's address is first planet from the Sun. Mercury is the planet closest to the Sun.

In the Solar System, *close* does not mean "right next to." Distances in space are very big.

Mercury's distance from the Sun is about 36 million miles.

If you went around the Earth 1,440 times, you would go 36 million miles.

Mercury is the smallest planet. It is not much bigger than our Moon. It looks a lot like the Moon, too. It is made of rock and metal.

Mercury's orbit is small. It takes only 88 Earth days to orbit the Sun. This is Mercury's year.

So a year on Mercury is 88 days. But a day on Mercury is very long, because Mercury rotates so slowly.

A day on Mercury is 59 Earth days.

Because it is so near the Sun, Mercury is hotter than you can imagine.

Venus

Venus is the second planet from the Sun. That is its address in the Solar System.

Its distance from the Sun is about 67 million miles. It is almost twice as far from the Sun as Mercury is. Venus is nearly the same size as Earth.

Earth

Venus

A year on Venus is about 225 Earth days, but a day on Venus is even longer. That's because Venus rotates so slowly.

Except for the Sun and Moon, Venus is the brightest object you can see in the sky. You can see it just after sunset or just before sunrise, when it looks like a very bright star.

Venus looks so bright because the thick clouds around it reflect a lot of sunlight. The clouds are poison gas. They keep Venus superhot.

We don't know all the reasons why Venus is so different from the Earth. It is almost Earth's twin in size, and they are next-door neighbors.

Earth

Planet Earth is where we live. Our address in the Solar System is third planet from the Sun.

The distance from the Sun is about 93 million miles.

Earth orbits the Sun in 365¼ days. That's a year on Earth.

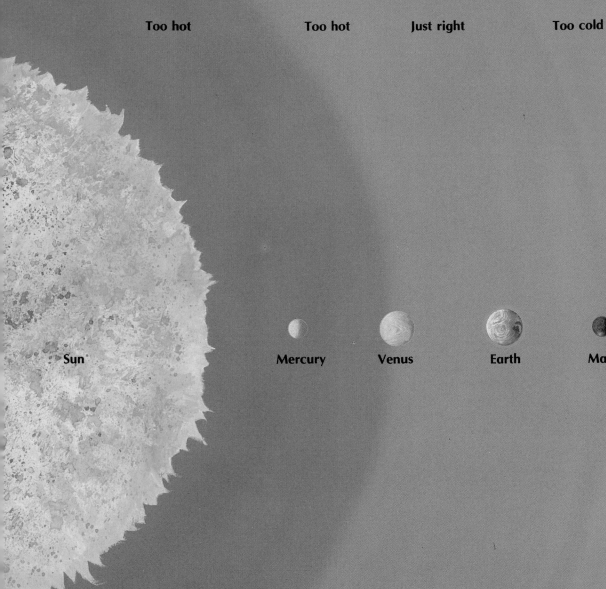

Too hot   Too hot   Just right   Too cold

Sun   Mercury   Venus   Earth   Mars

16

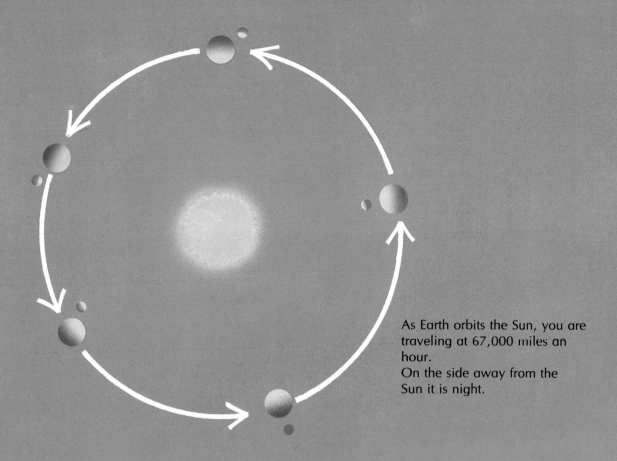

As Earth orbits the Sun, you are traveling at 67,000 miles an hour.
On the side away from the Sun it is night.

Earth is a special planet in the Solar System.

It is just the right distance from the Sun. It is warm enough for the water on Earth to stay liquid. If Earth were very hot, the water would boil away. If Earth were very cold, the water would freeze.

Earth has just enough gravity to hold the air that is around it.

18

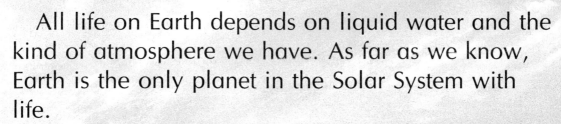

All life on Earth depends on liquid water and the kind of atmosphere we have. As far as we know, Earth is the only planet in the Solar System with life.

Earth has one big Moon. The Moon makes the tides on Earth.

Mars

Earth   Mars

Address in the Solar System: fourth planet from the Sun.

The distance from the Sun is about 141 million miles.

Mars is a little more than half the size of the Earth.

A year on Mars is almost twice as long as an Earth year. A day is only a little bit longer than an Earth day.

Mars has no atmosphere.

It has no liquid water.

Most of Mars is a red desert.

Mars has two very small moons. They look like big, lumpy rocks. They may actually have been asteroids that were captured by Mars' gravity long ago.

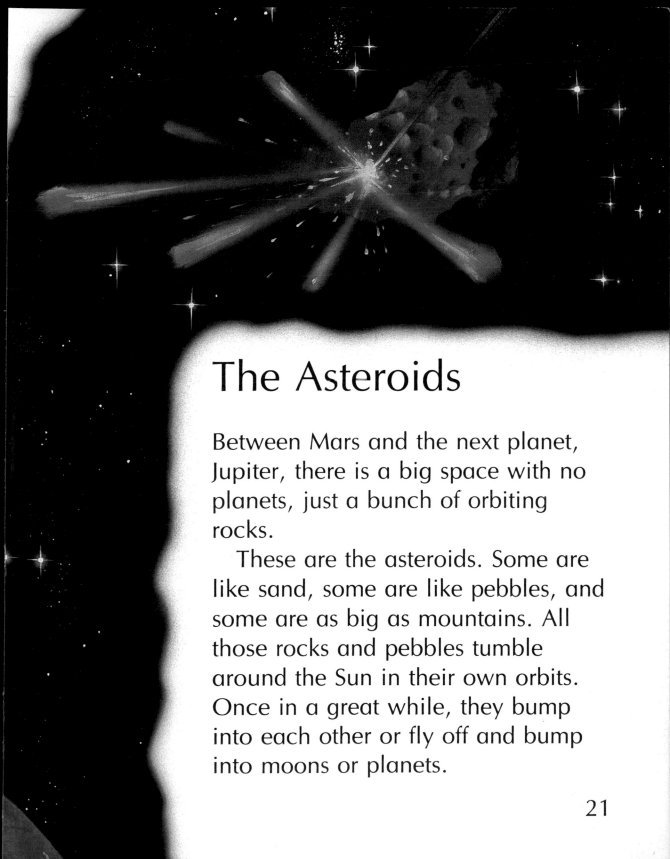

The Asteroids

Between Mars and the next planet, Jupiter, there is a big space with no planets, just a bunch of orbiting rocks.

These are the asteroids. Some are like sand, some are like pebbles, and some are as big as mountains. All those rocks and pebbles tumble around the Sun in their own orbits. Once in a great while, they bump into each other or fly off and bump into moons or planets.

Jupiter

Jupiter   **Earth**

Address in the Solar System:
fifth planet from the Sun.
The distance from the Sun is
about 483 million miles.

Jupiter is enormous. It's over eleven times bigger than Earth. Jupiter is bigger than all the other planets *combined.* Jupiter is a giant, but a very light giant. It is mostly a big gas ball.

A Jupiter year is almost twelve Earth years long. A Jupiter day is short, less than ten hours.

Jupiter looks striped. The stripes are bands of clouds. Small spots come and go on the stripes. One giant spot, called the **Great Red Spot,** is a storm larger than the Earth.

Jupiter has at least sixteen moons. Four of them are big and bright and about the size of our Moon or the planet Mercury.

One moon, Io, has volcanoes. Another moon, Ganymede, is the biggest moon in the Solar System, even bigger than the planet Mercury.

Jupiter and its moons are like a small Solar System. But Jupiter is not hot enough to burn like the Sun.

23

Saturn

Saturn's address: sixth planet from the Sun. Its distance from the Sun is 887 million miles.

Saturn is the second largest planet. It's over nine times bigger than the Earth. Saturn is another giant gas ball. In water, it would float! It's also very, very cold.

Saturn takes about 29½ Earth years to orbit the Sun. A day on Saturn is not quite eleven hours long.

Saturn's rings make Saturn special. The rings are made of dust and rocks and chunks of ice. The other giant planets have rings also, but Saturn has so many. Some of these are so big, you can see them through a small telescope. Some are wide. Some are narrow. Some are broken. Some are braided, like a girl's hair.

Saturn has at least twenty moons.
The largest moon, Titan, is bigger
than ours.

Titan

Earth

Uranus

Uranus

Address: seventh planet from the Sun.

The distance from the Sun is about 1.8 billion miles.

Compared with Earth, Uranus is a giant. But it's only a little more than a third the size of Jupiter.

Uranus is so far away from the Sun that if you were standing on Uranus, the Sun would look like a big, bright star.

The planets that are farther from the Sun have bigger orbits. They have a longer way to travel in their trip around the Sun. It takes eighty-four Earth years for Uranus to orbit the Sun. A day on Uranus is less than seventeen hours.

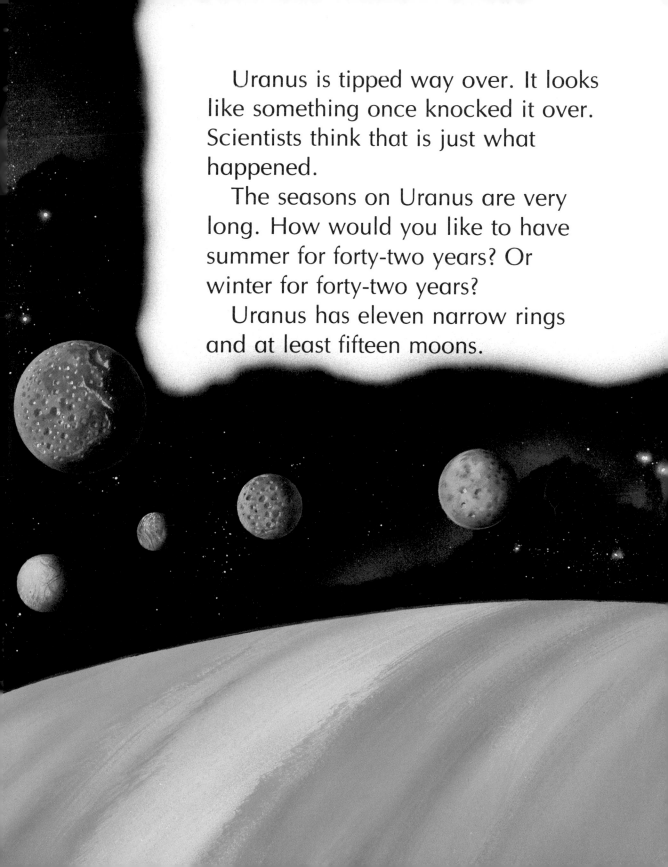

Uranus is tipped way over. It looks like something once knocked it over. Scientists think that is just what happened.

The seasons on Uranus are very long. How would you like to have summer for forty-two years? Or winter for forty-two years?

Uranus has eleven narrow rings and at least fifteen moons.

Neptune

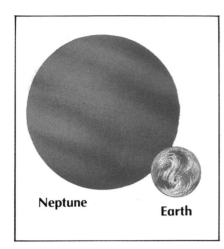

Neptune

Earth

Address: eighth planet from the Sun.

The distance from the Sun is about 2.8 billion miles.

Neptune is about the same size as Uranus.

Triton

A year on Neptune is 164 Earth years. A day is about fifteen hours long.

Neptune has eight moons. One, Triton, is about the same size as our Moon. Like Io, Triton has volcanoes.

Neptune looks blue. From space, Earth looks blue, too. That's because most of the Earth is covered with water. But Neptune is too cold to have liquid water. Neptune is blue because of a gas, called **methane,** in its atmosphere.

Pluto

Pluto

Earth

Pluto is usually the ninth planet from the Sun. But its orbit is so odd that sometimes it wanders closer to the Sun than Neptune. That is where it is now.

Pluto is about 3.6 billion miles from the Sun. A year on Pluto is almost 248 Earth years. A day on Pluto is as long as six Earth days.

Pluto is a quarter the size of the Earth. Some astronomers believe that Pluto was once a hunk of Neptune, or a moon of Neptune that escaped the planet's gravity.

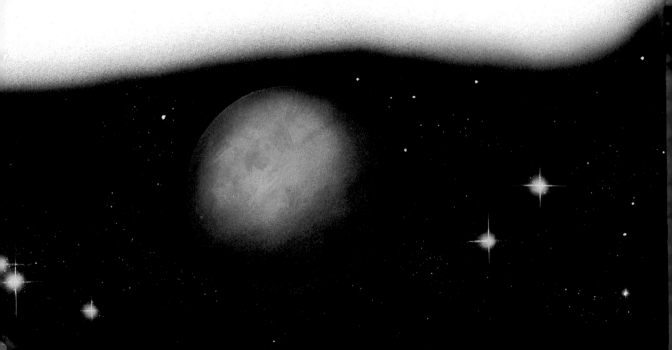

Is there another planet in the Solar System beyond Pluto? Astronomers are still looking. But as far as we know now, out past Pluto, there are only comets and then empty space, for billions and trillions of miles. Maybe someday people will travel there in spaceships to see what else they can find.

Index